Middle Stump

Middle Stump

AN ALPHABET OF CRICKETING TERMS
GRAHAM THOMPSON

Macdonald
Queen Anne Press

A *Queen Anne Press* BOOK

© Graham Thompson 1987
Introduction © Graham Gooch 1987

First published in Great Britain in 1987 by
Queen Anne Press, a division of
Macdonald & Co (Publishers) Ltd
3rd Floor
Greater London House
Hampstead Road
London NW1 7QX

A BPCC plc Company

British Library Cataloguing in Publication Data
Thompson, Graham
    Middle stump.
    1. Cricket—Anecdotes, facetiae,
    satire, etc.
    I. Title
    796.35'8'0207   GV919

    ISBN 0-356-12712-5

Typeset by York House Typographic Ltd
Printed and bound in Great Britain
by Purnell Book Production Limited
Member of the BPCC Group

Introduction
by Graham Gooch

A sense of humour is not a compulsory prerequisite of the modern cricketer. There are those to whom the game is far too serious a business ever to promote laughter. I feel sorry for them. They don't know what they are missing.

Cricket, more than any other sport, blends drama, tragedy and comedy with an element of the ridiculous. It is a sport which has rich pickings for the humorous writer and a bottomless well of material for the skilful cartoonist – a well into which Graham Thompson has dipped handsomely and hilariously in the following pages.

To me, a cricketer who cannot laugh, either at himself or at the comic mishaps of others, is a man of limited character. But then I freely admit I am fortunate. I have played all my county cricket with Essex and so I was brought up in a dressing-room atmosphere of light-hearted banter, of constant pranks and comic anecdotes. I have been there a long time now, but the laughter has never stopped.

There are days in the life of every player and every team when humour is a foreign emotion, entirely inappropriate to the solemn events occurring on or sometimes off the field; when the team heads for inevitable defeat, when a batsman collects his third successive 'duck' or when two teammates openly fall out – these are the occasions when the character of the players is put to the test. Paradoxically, these are also the times when a sense of humour is most essential. Break the ice, crack the maudlin faces into a grin or two and it is amazing how a crisis can recede.

I am convinced that the notorious manic humour of Essex players has been a major factor in our considerable successes over recent years. It must be remembered that a county cricket team spends an awful lot of time together – on the field, in dressing-rooms, in cars travelling up and down motorways between games, and in hotels. Business and social life is intermingled. You are similar to a family for the course of the season and, as in any family, life becomes very difficult if you don't get along with each other. Arguments never linger in our dressing-room. Of course, they do happen, we wouldn't be human if they didn't, but by the end of the day the quarrellers are invariably seeing the funny side of their dispute and the matter becomes material for yet another joke.

It helps that we have had a very constant personnel. Most of us have been with the county a good few years and when we do take on someone new it is always interesting to see how he reacts to the mickey-taking. I particularly remember Kenny McEwan when he joined us in 1974 as a replacement overseas player for the brilliant West Indian Keith Boyce. Kenny was only twenty-one and although he came with a good reputation from South Africa, it was plainly worrying him that he had a hard act to follow. He had a new bat for his debut and marched out with our good wishes in his ears. First ball, he edged the ball onto his pad and was given out lbw. Kenny couldn't believe it. Worse still, he just did not know how to face his new teammates. He trudged back, expected to be met by a critical silence and perhaps the odd carping comparison – and could hardly believe it when he opened the dressing-room door and found us all creased up laughing. Kenny was a quiet convert to Essex humour from that day on and, of course, became a magnificent servant of the county.

One year earlier, I had made my Essex debut in a side still captained by Brian Taylor. Known to all as 'Tonker', Brian had a sergeant-major's approach to the game and would bark out orders, knowing full well that he was causing considerable mirth in the ranks. One gloomy championship day on a deserted Midlands ground we were in the field and Keith Pont – then just twenty but already a comedian – was having to field at third man both ends. 'Ponty' eventually grew tired of running half-way round the ground after each over and, spotting an isolated spectator leaning on a push-bike, rapidly negotiated for its loan. 'Tonker', for once, was utterly lost for words as he looked up and saw the junior pro cycling around the boundary to get into position! It was a pity Graham Thompson was not present to capture the scene. There is a mixture of humour in our side from the laconic David Acfield to the outrageous antics of 'Ponty' and, of course, Ray East. Now retired to the sanctuary of coaching the second team, Ray will still regale anyone who asks with an amazing repertoire of stories, all superbly acted out. A nervous man by nature, he was a riot in the dressing-room and I remember him on our balcony waiting to go out and face West Indian fast bowler Malcolm Marshall. He donned a helmet and fitted two pieces of white paper into the holes on top so that they stuck out like the ears of a rabbit. If it was intended to encourage Marshall to take pity, it failed. Defending stylishly at the other end, Ray was out to the first ball he received from the great man. Back in the dressing-room he announced, 'I felt like Wally Hammond at one end and Donald Duck at the other!'

I could fill many more pages with reminiscences of Ray, 'Ponty' and the other comics, but the purpose of this introduction is simply to show an appreciation of what Graham Thompson is portraying. I have already laughed my way through his collection of cartoons, imagining myself and my team-mates in some of the semi-ludicrous yet disturbingly possible situations. It will lighten many a dark hour on rainy day county grounds around England.

Agricultural Shot

A wild slog – often the trademark of a tailender.

'That's the last bloody catch that fool of an under-gardener drops this season.'

Backing Up

In anticipation of a quick single, the non-striking batsman will 'back up' by walking down the wicket as the bowler delivers the ball.

'What do you mean let's run a third – I'm still on my first.'

Bouncers

Also called bumpers — fast short-pitched deliveries sometimes travelling at 90mph.

'This pair put me in mind of Lillee and Thomson.'
'Don't think I knew her, old chap.'

Box

A plastic shield worn by the batsman to preserve his deep voice. It is worn inside the trousers and gives confidence when faced with the menace of bouncing balls.

'What do you mean it smells, Gladstone – it fits down your trousers not on your head.'

Caught in the Slips

'The slips' is a hot catching position beside or slightly behind the wicketkeeper. Slip fielders are usually chosen for their lightning reflexes and safe hands.

'We're relieving you of the captaincy, Owlighter.'

Chinaman

A ball bowled by a left-hander which breaks from the off to the leg-side on bouncing, as viewed by a usually surprised right-handed batsman.

'That's the second time today that Cyril's been bowled by a Chinaman.'

Covers

Canvas sheets that cover the wicket in the event of rain.

'Dear Enid
    I have found this swell
spot in St John's Wood . . .'

Deep Third Man

A deep fielding position roughly 45° from the bat on the off side.

'Couldn't someone taller field here, Ponsonby?'

Duck

The batsman's nightmare – to score a duck is to score nought. To be bowled first ball is to score a golden duck.

'Well, that's a great start!'

Extras

Penalty runs given away by the fielding side, eg no-balls, leg-byes, byes or wides. These runs are not scored by the batsman.

'Bloke shouted "wide", and Mum thought he meant 'er.'

Fast Bowler

The spearhead of the bowling attack, a ruffler of batting feathers and a bouncer-out of batsmen.

'Be gentle with this new batsman, Tiger. I believe he's a tax collector.'

Fine leg

A fielding position just in from the boundary, fine leg stands at roughly 15° from the stumps.

''Er legs are all right but 'er drawers are a bit sticky.'

Forward Short Leg

*The closest fielding position to the batsman,
usually occupied by heroes and knuckleheads.*

Googly

A slow delivery by a right-handed bowler that breaks towards the leg-side of a right-handed batsman on bouncing, although it is delivered in the guise of a leg-break.

''E said right, fink you're so clever, bet you can't 'it my googlies . . .'

Hat-Trick

A bowler's dream – three wickets in a row.

'But I'm not carrying a truncheon WPC Fanshaw.'

Heavy Roller

One of the most important pieces of cricketing equipment. It is used by the groundstaff to roll the wicket and keep it flat, thus ensuring a predictable bounce of the ball.

'Remember Simkins, next time you employ a heavy roller make sure the grass hasn't just been cut.'

Hooker

A batsman who produces spectacular leg-side or rather earhole-side shots from a rising bouncing ball, usually resulting in six glorious runs or a 'skied' catch.

'Whip your bails off, dearie?'

Inside Edge

An involuntary batting stroke, the ball glancing off the inside edge of the bat.

'Next time that bugger gets an inside edge, inside that particular 'edge, 'e gets it 'imself.'

Jar

A receptacle for beer or cider – another name for a pint.

'Jus' one to steady the nerves, skip!'

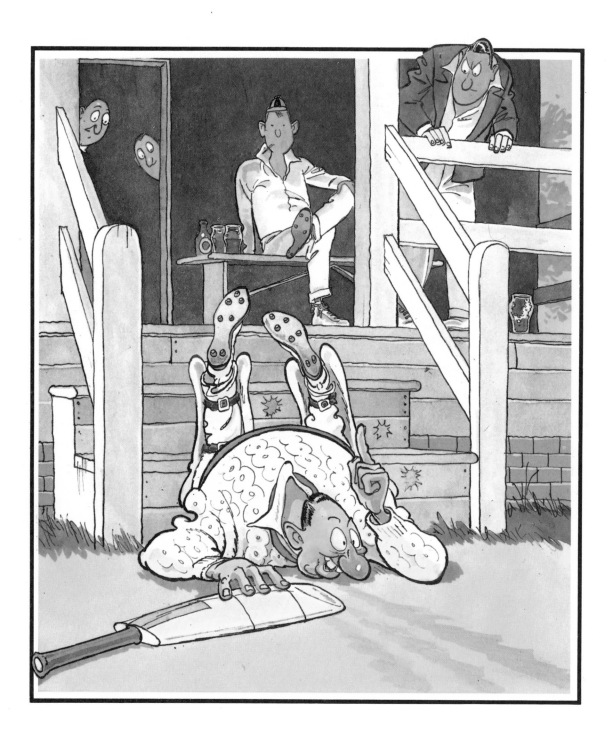

Knock

An innings.

'We can only hope it's not down to him to give the casting vote at your hearing, Guy.'

LBW

Leg before wicket. When a batsman is given out by the umpire because part of his body, usually his legs, have stopped or deflected a ball that would have struck the wicket.

'If the vicar insists on wearing one pad, I wish he would learn to put it on the right leg.'

Late Cut

*Good batsmen with time to play often employ
this delightful stroke, steering the ball between
gully and silly point.*

'If the committee would buy
a larger mower perhaps we
would get started on time,
Angus.'

Leg Glance

A glancing shot played between the
wicketkeeper and short square leg.

'Still one of life's little thrills,
Lady Parrotbill – the risky leg
glance.'

Light Meter

Used by photographers and umpires alike – a gauge for determining whether the light is good enough for safe play.

Light Roller

A lighter version of the heavy roller.

'Personally I would have chosen the light roller.'

Long Leg

Leg-side fielding position near the boundary, between deep fine leg and deep square leg.

'I think you should move your long leg in a bit closer, Miss Bulstrode.'

Middle Stump

The prized stump – the ultimate joy of any bowler is to watch the middle stump cartwheel through the air.

'I've found that box thingy of yours, Arnold!'

Maiden Over

An over in which no runs are scored.

'I hope you haven't got tuna
fish oil on my new bat,
Purvis.'

No-Ball

An illegal delivery called by the umpire, resulting in an extra run being added to the score of the batting side. If the batsman hits the ball he may run as though the delivery was legal. The usual cause of a no-ball is the bowler putting a foot over the crease in his run-up.

'He says he's ever so sorry he chewed your ball and he would like you to finish your game with his.'

Overthrow

This occurs when a ball is thrown in from a fielder and goes past the wicketkeeper thus allowing a further run or runs to be taken.

'Fine arm young Bellinger is developing, Headmaster.'

Outswinger

A ball which swings from the leg to the off-side stump when bowled.

'Still nibbling at the outswingers I see, Harrison!'

Padding Up

A batsman does this before walking to the wicket in order to protect his legs from the ball. Thigh pads and arm pads are also sometimes worn (mainly by sissies).

'Anyone seen the spare helmets?'

Quick Runs

Taken by batsmen who decide that they can get to the other end of the wicket before the fielders can retrieve the ball. Often they find they can't.

'He just cursed your brother's restaurant and ran.'

Rain

*A steady downpour or a Wagnerian
thunderstorm might stop a village cricket match.
A few drops of rain in the next county have been
known to send some Test cricketers scurrying to
the pavilion.*

'We'll have another
inspection at lunch time.'

Run-Up

Steps taken by a bowler before he delivers the ball. If a spinner or slow bowler he will only take a few steps but a genuine 'quickie' might start his run at the foot of the pavilion steps.

'And he's only de slow bowler, man!'

Square Leg

A fielding position in line with the batting crease on the on-side of the field.

'You've ironed my creams down the seams again, Muriel.'

Toss

Before the start of any match the respective captains will toss a coin. The one who calls correctly chooses whether to bat or field first.

'Looks like I win the toss, chaps.'

Taking Guard

On going to the wicket a batsman will choose a stump as a positional guide for his stand at the crease. He will place his bat upright in front of the selected stump and ask the umpire at the bowler's end if the chosen stump is correctly guarded by the bat.

'If you've finished familiarising yourself with the crease Tyttenhanger, we'll start the over.'

Umpire

An eagle-eyed paragon of virture or a short-sighted old twit depending on your point of view (fielder or batsman).

'Comes of signalling leg-byes with a wooden leg on a damp wicket.'

Vice-Captain

Second in command who takes over if the captain is injured or unavailable. A captain will often consult his vice when confronted with tricky decisions.

'Welcome to St Valkyries and let me put you in the capable hands of our vice-captain, Lucretia.'

Wicket Maiden

An over in which a wicket is taken without a run being scored.

'It's her Ladyship's contribution towards brighter cricket, Mellors.'

Xxx

Denotes the strength of the clubhouse beer or cider. Usually the precursor of one of cricket's favourite conditions – the half cut.

'And now Miss Kiri Te Kanawa takes her place with the massed choir.'

Yorker

A pretty lethal delivery which takes a lot of digging out and usually results in a desperate 'jarring' block as the batsman tries to prevent the ball from shooting under the bat.

'Careful our Cedric – I'm only in't carpet slippers.'

Zat!

A shortened version of the cry 'How's that' or 'Howzat', usually a frenzied appeal from the fielding side and its supporters demanding that the umpire gives the batsman out.

'God I hate these theatrical fixtures.'